Brightside 90-Day Goal Adventure Guide

HELEN FICKES

Edited by Andrew Fickes

For our daughter Jocelyn, our lil' Sweet Pea, tenacious explorer, and greatest inspiration

CONTENTS

1   Introduction to the Brightside 90-Day Goal Adventure   1

2   The Brightside 90-Day Goal Adventure Guide   2

3   Choosing Your 90-Day Goal   7

4   Brightside 90-Day Goal Adventure Road Map   8

5   How to Use Your Guide   12

6   30-Day Milestone   20

7   60-Day Milestone   48

8   Homestretch *(the final 30 days)*   76

9   Brightside 90-Day Goal Adventure Achieved!   105

Introduction to the Brightside 90-Day Goal Adventure

The Brightside 90-Day Goal Adventure is a transformative experience in which you **become the hero of your own story** and live a life filled with excitement, confidence and freedom. This adventure is like no other that you will take. On this journey you will **live inspired** while inspiring others. It is unique to you and your dreams. It celebrates the brave steps you take in exploration and discovery. Whether you are in search of better health, a career you love, financial abundance, or someone to enjoy life with; **you are ready to begin this quest**. Perhaps you imagine yourself owning a business, backpacking in Europe, or starting a family. The Brightside 90-Day Goal Adventure is your key to making your greatest desires a reality. By adopting the tools and resources within this guide, you are taking the first step toward living the life you have always wanted. Congratulations!!! Now, let's adventure together!!!

Preparing for Your Travels

When my husband and I got married we celebrated our new chapter in life by honeymooning along the stunning California coast. We started in gorgeous Santa Barbara, in a room with a view of the ocean. Our mornings began with delectable beignets and creamy lattes at the quaint corner cafe. We spent afternoons touring the sites by trolley and sailing along the sapphire waters. Evenings were enjoyed indulging in the local flavor and sipping on glasses of white wine.

After a few days in Santa Barbara we ventured north to Solvang, Monterey, and finally, San Francisco. We visited beaches, castles, aquariums, and, of course, the Golden Gate Bridge. Our California coast adventure is one that my husband and I speak of often, as it not only was spent with one another, but it is an experience that defined us and our story. We reflect upon our journey, remembering how it felt to reach our destination and what it took to get there. The reflection almost always leads us to contemplating the next expedition and the where, when, and how of it all. In playing with what is possible, we are already one step closer to bringing what we envision to life. For we have already "seen" the vacation paradise and believe that we will be there soon. It is what we imagine and what we bravely take on that contributes to feeling so *alive* and accomplishing what we want in life.

Our honeymoon was a much-needed excursion, and it was also a goal we set to achieve. My husband and I spent months before our trip preparing for our travels. There were several actions we had to take prior to our departure. We made decisions about where we wanted to go, when we wanted to get there, and what route would be best. We studied guidebooks and mapped out our journey. We made sure to save money and decided what to pack. We created our itinerary, invited others to share their suggestions about what to check out, and gathered resources we would need along the way. Most of all, we committed to the true purpose of our adventure, which was to relax and have fun together. In preparing for our honeymoon and taking the actions to achieve our goal, we got the most out of our experience and enjoyed something amazing!

I want the same for you – to *experience something amazing*, something that makes you feel as though you are taking advantage of every single moment this life has to offer. I invite you to approach your Brightside 90-Day Goal Adventure with the same excitement and preparation you would apply toward any of your travels. Choose where you want to be and the purpose for your journey. Know what you want to achieve and why it is important to you to do so. Immerse yourself in the vision of what life will look like once you have accomplished your goal. Imagine what you will do once you reach your destination. Prepare for your travels and plan the best way to get there. Develop an action plan (also known as an itinerary). Gather all of those things you will need for your journey and get excited!!! Where will *this* Adventure take you? There is only one step left – *start the quest*!

The Brightside 90-Day Goal Adventure Guide

…for the inspired and the inspiring…

Your Brightside 90-Day Goal Adventure Guide is set up like a travel journal of sorts, giving you a chance to note your path, tell your tale, and revel in your heroism and bravery. Your Guide is all about you, your goals, your dreams, and your desires. It is for the inspired and the inspiring!!! It will help you focus, get organized, get motivated, and, of course, achieve your 90-Day Goal.

As you set out on your journey, it is important to assess the tools within your pack. Each resource is essential to the quest and will be further developed along the way. Your Guide will lead you to define your *purpose*, play with *possibility*, focus on *positivity*, develop a *plan*, organize your *priorities*, and welcome encouraging *partners* to the journey.

Purpose

"Respond to every call that excites your spirit."
Rumi

A few years ago, I attended a writing workshop given by Tama Kieves, author of "This Time I Dance" and "A Year Without Fear." She had released her first book not too long prior and was sharing her story about her journey from Harvard lawyer to published writer. I was inspired by her intense desire to live out a dream that she had since she was a little girl. She was an example of what it looked like to achieve your goals and live with purpose.

Attending the workshop was a defining moment in my life. The experience led me to acknowledge and define what I was meant to do. I wanted to inspire others through my writing. The workshop resonated with me because writing is part of my purpose and once I started living with purpose, my journey took on a life of its own.

Imagine if Tama Kieves had not lived with purpose. Imagine if I did not live *my* life with purpose. Now, imagine the impact *you* make when you live your life with purpose. Defining our purpose and following the proposed path is not always easy. Sometimes it is difficult to determine why you are doing something. Is it because of what you want, or is it to please someone else? It is a good idea to check in with yourself before and throughout your Adventure to make sure that you are in pursuit of what serves you and your best self. If you ever find the Adventure is turning into an expedition that is not about you and your goals, ask what you can do to get back on track. There are several reflection exercises within the Guide to help you check in and lead you back to your path.

To help you define your purpose, ask yourself:

- What excites your spirit?
- What does that inner voice keep saying?
- What makes accomplishing your 90-Day Goal so important?
- What will it look and feel like once you have reached your destination?

Discovering and defining your purpose for this journey is the first step toward clear direction and focus. Specific goals and action steps will soon follow because your goals are a reflection of your purpose and what is important to you. Your purpose can be anything, as long as it is true for you. Your purpose is why you are on this Adventure and your goal is what you need to accomplish to fulfill this purpose. For example, if your purpose is to be a healthier person, then your 90-Day Goal may be to lose 15 pounds. Perhaps you are seeking greater freedom or financial abundance. Your 90-

Day Goal may be to launch your own business. Maybe you are in search of a meaningful experience and going to Europe for the summer becomes your 90-Day Goal. Whatever your purpose for this Adventure may be, you will know that you are on the right path because you will feel inspired, energized, and have an intense desire to reach the destination.

Possibility

"There are no limitations to the mind except those we acknowledge."
Napoleon Hill

Your Adventure requires you to be a dreamer and a believer, for every achievement begins when one has the courage to imagine what is possible, and we are only ready to receive such success when we believe that what is possible can happen to *us*.

Imagining what is possible and playing with those possibilities is the essence of your Adventure. When you take an adventure in possibility, you open yourself up to a wealth of creative ideas and opportunities. Some possibilities will be outlandish and others will be safe, and yet every imagined scenario will help lead you to a new experience, solutions and perspective.

Achieving your 90-Day Goal may require you to change or adopt a new perspective. I heard this story once about a couple who went camping by this beautiful lake. Only, they could not see the lake because they had parked their Winnebago right along the bank, blocking their view. On the first day of their trip they sat outside in their camping chairs staring at the vehicle, not realizing the beauty on the other side. On the second day of their trip a passer-by asked if they had enjoyed the lake yet. They asked, "What lake?" The passer-by said, "It is just behind your Winnebago." The couple had no idea and wondered what they needed to do to enjoy the beauty on the other side of their obstacle. They moved their chairs to the left but could only see part of the picturesque view. They moved their chairs to the right and were able to see the view from a slightly different angle, but they still could not get a full sense of the beauty before them. They grew frustrated and went back inside the Winnebago. On the third day of their trip the passer-by came back to them and asked if they had enjoyed the lake yet. They explained that they tried, but it was just not possible to see the whole lake from where they were located. They were disappointed to be missing out. The passer-by suggested, "What if you moved the Winnebago?" The couple thought about it for a minute and said, "Why, that's a great idea!!!"

In the story of the Winnebago, the couple was finding it difficult to imagine all of the possibilities available to them and, in doing so, struggled to change their perspective and accomplish what they wanted to. The Winnebago was the challenge and the possibilities were solutions to help meet that challenge. If you find that you are struggling to figure out how to achieve your goal or get past an obstacle, I invite you to spend about 10 minutes brainstorming as many possibilities as you can imagine. Walk around the Winnebago, if you will, to change your perspective. Move the Winnebago even, out of sight and out of mind. Imagine if the challenge was not there, what actions would you take then to accomplish what you wanted to? Do not worry about whether a possibility is feasible or not. Just write it down and play with the possibility. If you get stuck, think about your role models who play with possibility. For example, Tama Kieves was a role model for me. She played with the possibility of going from Harvard lawyer to author, and in doing so found happiness and served as an example that such a thing can happen. You can also ask someone for help. The couple had the passer-by to offer a solution. You may have friends and family who can do the same. There is beauty in the Adventure for you to enjoy. Adventure in possibility, change your perspective, and see what comes from your bravery to try something new.

Positivity

"The world of achievement has always belonged to the optimist."
J. Harold Wilkins

To achieve, we must first believe! Successful outcomes start first in our mind. Our thoughts, whether they are positive or negative, influence our actions and our actions influence our reality. It is simple: if you are seeking positive outcomes, fill your mind with positive thoughts.

You will be invited often to write down your 90-Day Goal. Write it and think about it as though you have already achieved the goal, and be detailed in your vision. For example, say you want to learn how to play the guitar. Instead of saying, "I will know how to play the guitar by the end of my Brightside 90-Day Goal Adventure," say, "I am a musician. People request that I play my guitar for them often and I love it! I may even start teaching lessons!" Within this reiteration, and acting as if you are already where you desire to be, your subconscious, that part of our mind that influences our actions and feelings, believes in what you tell it more and more. Your subconscious then begins to translate what it believes into fact and the only outcome that makes sense is the one supported by those facts.

In addition to writing down your 90-Day Goal often, speak it out loud twice daily: when you wake up, and before you go to sleep. Again, speak in the present tense and with emotion so as to reinforce the successful outcome. Truly visualize the life you lead now. Allow your imagination to run free and believe in your ability to accomplish what you set out to do, for what is in your heart is meant to be achieved. Feel the glory of your accomplishment. Step into the victory. Explore the world of achievement. Repetition of our goals is all about fueling and refueling the mind with positive thought as we drive toward an inspired and inspiring horizon, on our way to rising above it all!

Plan

"Don't search for inspiration when you have a task to do; **Just start** *your work and you will see that it will soon find you."*
Charles Ghigna

When you go anywhere, whether it be on a cross-country drive or to the local coffeehouse, you need to know how to get there, right? Sure, you may be on autopilot to the coffeehouse now, but the first time you went there you had to know how to find it. You gathered the information you needed to get there, and you set out on your way with direction and most likely an intense desire…albeit for caffeine. Figuring out how to reach the destination of your Brightside 90-Day Goal Adventure is similar. You will need a set of directions and, though I joke about the caffeine, you will also need that intense desire to reach your journey's end.

That intense desire is fueled by your purpose, and your action plan serves as your trail map on this expedition. In detailing a list of what it takes to achieve your 90-Day Goal and defining when those steps will be taken on your Adventure, you gather a better sense of where you are headed, while also being able to document your progress.

Mapping out your journey also provides advanced notice of the course ahead. The passage may include some treacherous ravines. Being aware of possible challenges will give you an opportunity to prepare to conquer them. This preparation ignites an ambition that will carry you to the end.

As you develop your plan, remember the most important step: ***take action***. It is one thing to know what to do. It is another thing to do it, for knowledge only has value once it has been applied. In his book "Outliers," Malcolm Gladwell informed that it takes 10,000 hours of *working toward something* to master it. Know that goals are not accomplished overnight. Nor should they be. Goals that lead to a purposeful journey and substantial success take time, commitment and consistent action to achieve. So, whether you have 10 minutes or an hour, make sure that you are investing time every day to move your plan into action and to work on your 90-Day Goal. Use your Guide, as it is essential to your Adventure and *will* lead you to where you wish to be with an intensity that will propel you forward.

Prioritize

"The key is not to prioritize what's on your schedule, but to schedule your priorities."
Stephen Covey

Though it is important to your Adventure to dream BIG, think BIG, and to generally let go of limitations, there is one limitation that will work for you. That limitation is time. Factoring the element of time into goal-setting is beneficial because it adds a sense of urgency to completing the mission. Why wait any longer to achieve what it is that is in your heart? A time-based goal inspires prompt, definite decisions - the opposite of procrastination.

Prompt, definite decisions based on your purpose are key elements to success, as is the ability to prioritize. For example, when you go on a trip, do you do everything there is to do in that city or town? That would only be possible if you had an unlimited amount of time. So, you prioritize the various activities, organize a plan, and set out on your way.

Your Brightside 90-Day Goal Adventure provides just enough time to accomplish something great, but not so much time that it allows you to rest along the Lazy River or walk aimlessly without an end in sight. It gets you moving, and with purpose! When we are in action, we are making things happen. By going on this Adventure you are not only building a life that will bring greater freedom and more fulfillment, you are also prioritizing you and your desires. How wonderful is that? Use your Guide's *Weekly Itinerary* to prioritize your activities, get things done, and keep you at the center of your story.

Partners

"Surround yourself with the dreamers & the doers, the believers & the thinkers, but most of all surround yourself with those who see the greatness within you even when you don't see it yourself."
Edmund Lee

Embark on this journey with those who will lift you up. It makes a difference to be able to share your experiences, both good and bad, with those who support, encourage, and are genuinely interested in your story and celebrating your success. Your travel partners are your greatest motivational resource. They are the people that are celebrating all of your achievements, no matter how large or small, and reminding you to do so as well. They are the friends, the family, the colleagues, and the coaches that are picking you up along the way when you face fatigue, get overwhelmed, or simply need a boost. They live in the excitement of your journey alongside you and believe in what you are about to accomplish. They shout along the path, "You can do it!" because they *know* you can.

Your encouraging travel partners are also the people that will keep you accountable. Now, please be selective in choosing your travel partners. There is a difference between accountability and discouragement, or lack of belief. You will want to choose travel partners that are harmonious with your purpose and goals. Do not invite those on your journey that are not in alignment with your values and instead impose their own limitations on you. The limitations set by others are a reflection of the limitations they set on themselves. They are not true for you. Accountability is an entirely different way of working. It is a way to track your progress by including those travel partners on your expedition that ask what worked, what did not work, and what you will do to make it better. They will help you get back on the path when you have wavered. It happens to the best of us, but *you* will not have to worry about finding your way again because you have established a great support network that will provide hope when you most need it. They will share in your success, because your success matters just as much to them as it does to you. Gather those encouraging travel partners before and during your journey.

In addition to gathering encouraging travel partners that you already know, join or start an accountability group before you begin your travels. Accountability groups serve as an amazing resource for achieving your goals. For one, they enhance your success by providing a community you can

As a Brightside 90-Day Goal Adventurer, you have become part of a very special community of like-minded "dreamers, doers, believers, and thinkers." A Facebook accountability group, the Brightside 90-Day Goal Adventurers, has been set up especially for all of you. To join the group, go to the following link: https://www.facebook.com/groups/Brightside90DayGoalAdventurers/. You will need to log into your Facebook account or create one at www.facebook.com. Click on "Join Group." Once you receive confirmation, tell us about your 90-Day Goal and what we can do to best support you in your journey. You are welcome to check in and post daily, a couple of times a day, every other day, or whatever will most benefit you. You are invited to ask questions, offer encouragement, and share your wins, opportunities, steps to success, milestones, celebrations, and more.

learn from as well as contribute to. These groups are made up of those who are also working toward achieving their own goals – sometimes the goal is quite similar to yours. With everyone having a common purpose, the support is that much greater. Accountability groups also serve as a source of accumulated knowledge and can help answer questions you may have, inspire possibilities and solutions, and connect you with opportunities aligned with your vision as you move forward in your travels.

Now let's begin your Brightside 90-Day Goal Adventure!!!

Choosing Your 90-Day Goal

Now it is time to figure out where you are going on this Adventure by choosing your 90-Day Goal. You may already have your 90-Day Goal figured out. If so, feel free to jump forward to the *Brightside 90-Day Goal Adventure Road Map*. However, maybe you need to develop your 90-Day Goal more or make a choice among a number of aspirations. If this is the case, I invite you to try the Dream Life exercise below to decide on the focus of *this* Adventure. Remember, you can always take another Adventure once this one is complete. In fact, I strongly encourage it!

Dream Life Exercise

Earlier I spoke of my California coast getaway with my husband. Though we loved every moment of the trip, we found Santa Barbara to be especially wonderful and have made a goal to return there again very soon. What made it so fantastic was that for three days we had the opportunity to live this Dream Life. We could do anything we wanted and be anyone we wanted to be. We imagined what it would be like if we lived in Santa Barbara and thought about what we would do, how we would spend our time, and more. Nestled within that vision were many aspirations. We imagined a beautiful home on the beach. That's a goal. We talked about spending our days as published writers and successful business owners of a coffeehouse. Those are goals. Of course to live in Santa Barbara, it would be best to be financially abundant. Yet, another goal.

Now, imagine a fantastic vacation you have taken or would like to take. Where would you go? Who is on the adventure with you? How would you spend your time? Now, close your eyes and consider what it would be like if that vacation was your life. What do you see? How do you feel? What is it that you are enjoying? Have fun dreaming BIG!

Next, write down the answers to the questions above, and whatever else is part of creating your Dream Life. An example can be found in the text box to the right. You may also choose to create a vision board (a collage of images showing what you are striving for) with some magazines and poster board or on Pinterest (www.pinterest.com), if that works better for you.

> My Dream Life example:
>
> - Live in Santa Barbara, CA with my family.
> - Own a home on the beach.
> - Write for a living.
> - Own and operate a coffeehouse.
> - Become financially abundant.

You will note that there are several insights within your vision that show what you want and value. These desires provide an idea of your goals. What goals do you pick out from your Dream Life exercise? Of those aspirations, pick out three insights that match what you are looking to achieve at this point in your life. Of those three goals, which goal excites you most? What can you work toward right now? For example, within my list I mentioned a desire to write for a living. This is something that I have always wanted to do, which is why it was part of my Dream Life exercise. The thought of becoming a published writer is both exciting and something that fit into what I was looking to achieve at that point in my life. So, becoming a published writer became my 90-Day Goal.

Once you have chosen your 90-Day Goal make sure that it is challenging enough to push you beyond your comfort zone, and yet achievable within a 90-day period. If it isn't challenging enough, how can you kick it up a notch? If it isn't achievable in 90 days, how can you break it down? Returning to my 90-Day Goal of becoming a published writer, I would love to be on the New York Times Bestseller list. However, I understand that writing a New York Times Bestseller is not necessarily achievable in 90 days. However, what *could* I do in 90 days? I could create an idea, develop it, and publish something! This goal is both challenging and achievable. Hence, the Brightside 90-Day Goal Adventure Guide was born. If your goal is challenging, and yet achievable, fantastic! You are ready to move on in this journey.

Brightside 90-Day Goal Adventure Road Map

1. What is your 90-Day Goal?

2. What makes accomplishing this 90-Day Goal important to you? What will achieving *this* goal bring forth for you?

3. What date will you start your 90-Day Goal?

4. When will you accomplish your 90-Day Goal?

5. What specific tasks will you have accomplished by the end of the 90-Day period?

6. How will you know you have been successful?

7. What are two milestones (mini-goals) that you will achieve in 30 and 60 days that will contribute to the larger 90-Day Goal?

8. What resources will you need and/or what steps will you need to put into place to achieve your 90-Day Goal? For example, adopt a new perspective, build your support network, hire someone, get a partner's support, take a class, etc.?

9. What resources do you already have that will help you reach your 90-Day Goal?

10. Who are your primary supporters? Brainstorm your list. Do not worry if you only have one or two people or even if you are your only cheerleader. I guarantee you will add more as you progress toward achieving your 90-Day Goal.

11. What might get in the way of you achieving your 90-Day Goal?

12. What steps will you take to keep yourself on track?

13. How will you reward yourself for achieving your 90-Day Goal?

14. Make a commitment. What action(s) will you take now, before the first day of your journey, that will reflect and ensure your accomplishment of your 90-Day Goal? For example, if your 90-Day Goal is to complete your memoir, you can presell your book for the date it will be released. If you are striving to lose 15 pounds, you can schedule a photo shoot on the day after your Adventure is complete.

Fill in the blanks:

My 90-Day Goal is to _answer #1_, within the period of _answer #3_ and _answer #4_. It is important for me to achieve my 90-Day Goal because _answer #2_. I will know that I have been successful in achieving my 90-Day Goal when _answer #5_.

My 90-Day Goal is to…

Congratulations, you are off to a great start! Continue on the path to success by completing these action steps within the first week of your Brightside 90-Day Goal Adventure.

- ✓ Complete the *Brightside 90-Day Goal Adventure Road Map*
- ☐ Join the Brightside 90-Day Goal Adventurers Facebook accountability group at https://www.facebook.com/groups/Brightside90DayGoalAdventurers/ and check in as often as works best for you. For greater results, consider hiring a personal success coach.
- ☐ For additional support, resources and opportunities:
  - o "Like" the Brightside Business & Career Coaching Facebook page at https://www.facebook.com/brightsidecareer?ref=hl.
  - o Follow Brightside Business & Career Coaching on Instagram at https://instagram.com/brightsidecareer/.
  - o Check out www.brightsidecareer.com.
- ☐ Share your 90-Day Goal and when you will achieve it with 1-2 encouraging travel partners and/or the Brightside 90-Day Goal Adventurers accountability group.
  - o Continue to add encouraging travel partners to your list of primary supporters and share your 90-Day Goal with them as well. Ask for their help in checking in with you from time to time so that you may share your progress.
- ☐ Surround yourself with the people and things that inspire you and motivate you to take action.
- ☐ Make the commitment!
- ☐ Enjoy the Adventure!

How to Use Your Guide

Your Guide is made up of five main parts:

- *Milestone and Homestretch Action Plans:* Detail within the *Milestone Action Plans* the steps you will take to reach your 30-Day and 60-Day Milestones to bring you closer to reaching your 90-Day Goal. The *Homestretch Action Plan* consists of the final 30 days, in which you will plan the actions you need to take on the last leg of your Adventure.
- *Weekly Itinerary:* Schedule your priorities, boost your confidence, and get inspired.
- *7-Day Reflections:* Look back over the last seven days to share your wins, opportunities, and what you will do to make the next seven days even more successful.
- *30-Day* and *60-Day Milestone Reflections:* Look back at the last 30-day segment to note what you have learned and how you can apply your knowledge to the next 30 days, creating a more solid foundation for meeting your 90-Day Goal.
- *90-Day Goal Reflection* and *Travel Writer Challenge:* Congratulations! You have arrived at your final destination. To complete the Adventure, continue the practice of reflection and really celebrate how far you have come. This reflection will also help prepare you for the next Adventure when you are ready to take it. *(Travel Warning: The Brightside 90-Day Goal Adventure is addictive!!!)* The *Travel Writer Challenge* is your opportunity to share your success with others. Have fun with it! You have done an amazing job and you will be sure to inspire others with your story.

Milestone and Homestretch Action Plans

At the beginning of every 30-day segment, you will have an opportunity to choose a milestone and detail within the *Action Plans* those steps you will commit to within the next 30 days to help you reach your larger 90-Day Goal. The *Action Plans* will help provide direction, focus and motivation as well as help you assess whether you are going to reach your 90-Day Goal much quicker than expected, you are on track to complete your Adventure within the 90 days, or you need to speed up your progress. Your *Homestretch Action Plan* makes up the final 30 days of your Adventure and will be your last push needed to conquer the quest.

If, before or within the 30-Day Milestone, it looks as though you are going to reach the end of your Adventure quicker than expected, go back to your 90-Day Goal and assess whether the quest is too easy. Maybe you need to take it to the next level. Are you taking all of the necessary steps or are you allowing yourself to take shortcuts? Be honest with yourself about this. If you are investing less than 100 percent into this journey, ask yourself what needs to change for you to feel motivated to give it your all. Are you excited about reaching the destination? If not, what would bring you more excitement? Update your 90-Day Goal accordingly.

Then again, if, before or within the 30-Day Milestone, you experience the opposite scenario and fear that you may not reach your 90-Day Goal within the specified timeframe, go back to your 90-Day Goal and ask yourself if the quest is too hard. You definitely want the goal to be challenging, and yet achievable. If you need to take some extra steps and break the goal down even more that is okay, as long as you are still reaching a few steps outside your comfort zone. Ask yourself what needs to change to reach your destination. It may be that you just need to invest more time into working toward your goal.

Your *Action Plans* include five areas of focus: *the basics, action steps, potential challenges, investing in your travel partners,* and the *milestone achievement reward.*

- *The Basics:* Within the first section, indicate the start date and end date of your milestone. Then, write what you will accomplish at the end of the 30-day segment to help you in achieving the larger 90-Day Goal.
- *Action Steps:* Within the action steps, brainstorm all the steps that need to be taken to complete the 30-day/60-day milestone or homestretch (the final 30 days). You will refer to these action steps when you complete a similar section within your *Weekly Itinerary*. Feel free to continue to add to the action steps as you deem necessary and make sure to check off the action steps as you complete them. If there are action steps that still need to be completed, transfer them to the action steps within the next *Action Plan*.
- *Potential Challenges:* This next section provides an opportunity to identify potential challenges or roadblocks that may present themselves within the next 30 days. This awareness sets you up for success because it gives you adequate time to prepare, play with possibilities, develop solutions, and plan for the challenge.
- *Investing in Your Travel Partners:* Just as it is important to your success to invite encouraging travel partners to participate in your Adventure, it is essential for you to be an encouraging travel partner for others also and invest in your community. Note when fellow travel partners may be celebrating an accomplishment or special event, what that accomplishment or event may be, and the step(s) you will take to honor and support those who support you. Be sure to mark these important dates and events in your *Weekly Itinerary*.
- *Milestone Achievement Reward:* What will you do to celebrate your 30-day/60-day milestone accomplishment? Have fun thinking up a reward that reflects your hard work and achievement. If you prefer, feel free to use this space to creatively show how you will reward yourself - maybe with a photo, image, or doodle.

Example of Action Plan:

30-Day Milestone Action Plan			
Start date of milestone:	May 2, 2015	End date of milestone:	May 31, 2015

Within the next 30 days I will:
Write an outline of what I want to include in my Guide, write the first draft, and have my husband Andrew, also my editor, proofread the copy.

To accomplish my 30-Day Milestone, I will take the following action steps:	
✓	Brainstorm ideas to include in the Guide
✓	Flesh out those ideas by researching the concepts and add new ideas as I learn more
	Write the outline
	Follow the outline as I write the first draft
	Complete first draft and give to Andrew for editing

Events that may challenge me in successfully completing my 30-Day Milestone include:
Lots of celebrations coming up within the month of May – graduation, Mother's Day, birthdays. My weekends are completely filled, which will present a time challenge.

I will take the following actions to face and conquer these potential challenges and roadblocks:
Schedule and commit to one hour every evening after having dinner with my family to work on the Guide. Schedule and commit to two hours every Saturday from 7-9am to work on the Guide at the local coffeehouse.

Special dates and events coming up within the next 30 days for my encouraging travel partners and supporters include:			
Partner/Supporter	Date	Event	To-Do
Lily	May 15, 2015	Two interviews scheduled, 30-Day Milestone	Wish luck before interview, congratulate after, find out how they went
Andrew	May 21, 2015	Birthday	Enjoy a day of celebration and surprises

I will reward myself for achieving my 30-Day Milestone in the following way:
Date night with my husband, dinner, and a show!!!

Weekly Itinerary

Following the *Action Plans*, there will be 30 days-worth of itineraries in which you will schedule goal-focused and everyday activities, track your action steps, boost your confidence, get a little inspiration, and more. You will quickly note that days are free of specifics other than "Day 1...2...3" and so forth. The purpose of this is to encourage you to **start your Adventure now** and not wait another second. To stay organized, there are spaces for you to fill in the dates of the corresponding calendar week as well as the calendar date and day of the week themselves.

In addition to the daily planner, the *Weekly Itinerary* features:

- *Today I Will*: Commit to three actions you will complete each day and strive to accomplish these mini-goals as early in the day as possible. There are only three rules: 1) Choose *no more than* three actions to focus on each day. 2) At least one action must be from your *7-Day Action Steps*. If you have completed all of your *7-Day Action Steps*, choose an action from your *Action Plan*. 3) Fill this section out in advance, ideally the night before.
- *90-Day Goal*: Take special note of this section which invites you to write down your 90-Day Goal. You may question why it is that I ask you to write your 90-Day Goal within every *Action Plan* as well as every seven days. There is a purpose. Simply in writing down your goals once, it is proven that you come closer to achieving the goal. Now, imagine what you can achieve, to what degree, and how quickly you can make it happen if you keep the goal at the forefront of your mind. With every stroke of the pen, you are reiterating the importance of achieving your goal. You are fueling and refueling your mind to believe in no other outcome but a successful one and act upon it. You are building a habit of positive thinking.
- *7-Day Action Steps*: Choose four action steps from your *Action Plan* to focus on every seven days. As you complete the actions, check them off within your *7-Day Action Steps* as well as within your *Action Plan*. These actions may be practiced daily or once in the 7-day period. For example, if you are trying to eat healthier, your action step may be to skip sugar daily. This action step will be practiced every day within the 7-day period. A second action step may be a one-time action, such as you will cook a healthy meal at home at least once within the 7-day period.
  - Within the last two days of each 30-day segment, you will notice that you are given the opportunity to choose more than four action steps. Take this opportunity to indicate only those actions that you must complete within the next two days to reach your milestone or achieve your 90-Day Goal.
  - If you find that you are listing more action steps than you have time for, assess whether the quest is too big to achieve within 90 days or whether you need to invest more time in working toward your goal over the next 30-day period. This may be the time to utilize the resources of your accountability group.
  - *Note of Self-Compassion:* As you move forward in your Brightside 90-Day Goal Adventure make sure to celebrate your steps toward success while also showing yourself compassion during those times in which it may take you a little more time than expected to achieve a certain result. There may be times when you are struggling to find that motivation you had at the beginning of the journey, especially when the experience may not look like you thought it would. Show yourself compassion and look to your encouraging travel partners for support. Realize that there is no such thing as failure when you are consistently working toward your goals and doing your best. If anything, just by taking the steps you already have, you are that much closer than you were before to reaching your destination. That is something to be proud of!
- *Inspirational Quotes*: There are so many amazing people out there to inspire us with their creativity, insight and perspective. Learn from them. Listen to how they develop and define their positive, success mindset. Peppered throughout your Guide you will find inspirational

quotes with the intention to expand upon your current state of thought, motivate you, and inspire you to higher levels.

- *Confidence Booster Challenges:* To achieve, you must first believe! Building your confidence will help in building your belief, so that you will not only accomplish your 90-Day Goal but also show yourself the many other things you are capable of. The *Confidence Booster Challenge* will energize you as you step outside your comfort zone and focus on conquering the *Challenge.* Practice the *Confidence Booster Challenge* each of the seven days and use the *Confidence Booster Challenge Journal,* located after the *Weekly Itinerary,* to complete the quest and record your related *Insights & Inspirations.*

- *Motivational Resources I Love!:* What motivates you? Every adventure has its highs and lows and spending time on your journey to think about what motivates you will prepare you for when you need a boost of encouragement, inspiration, or to kick it up a notch. As you move through the Adventure and grow inspired by the books, music, online treasures, role models, inspirational quotes, and so forth you discover along the way, note these resources within the *Motivational Resources I Love!* and tap into those resources whenever and as much as you need to.

- *Insights & Inspirations:* You have some incredible ideas, and you will also discover wonderful gems of wisdom along the way. You are an inspired and inspiring individual! It is important to note all of those quick insights that pass through your mind at any given moment. You'll know when you have discovered a golden nugget of inspiration or opportunity, as you'll feel it in your bones. Write it down! Draw it out! Do not dismiss it! Our best ideas are born from these sudden impulses of thought, playing with possibility, and giving our imagination free reign. There are plenty of opportunities throughout the Guide to note your *Insights & Inspirations.* It is up to you how you record them. The space is yours to do what you will – write, draw, paint, collage, add photos, do whatever pleases the creative, adventurous being that you are!

Example of Weekly Itinerary:

Week of:		May 2-8, 2015					
Day 1		**Day 2**		**Day 3**		**Day 4**	
W	May 2	Th	May 3	F	May 4	S	May 5
6a							
7a	30 min workout			30 min workout			
8a						Coffee with Lily, ask about goals	
9a	Schedule times for writing	Brainstorm ideas and concepts				Writing focus time	
10a	Brainstorm ideas and concepts	Writing focus time		Writing focus time		Writing focus time	

Today I Will:							
X	Schedule writing focus times	X	Brainstorm ideas	X	1hr writing focus	X	Coffee with Lily - goals
X	30 min workout	X	Take Jocelyn to the park	X	Send congrats card to Collin	X	2 hrs writing focus
X	Clean house	X	Pay electric bill	X	30 min workout		Oil change

90-Day Goal

I am the published author of the *Brightside 90-Day Goal Adventure Guide*, which helps people get focused, get organized, get motivated, and achieve their goals.

7-Day Action Steps	
1	Schedule and commit to an hour daily of writing focus time
2	Schedule and commit to two hours this Saturday of writing focus time
3	Brainstorm ideas and concepts that I want to include in the Guide
4	Ask friends and family about their goals and what they do to achieve them

7-Day Reflection

Founder of Analytical Psychology, Carl Jung once said, "Your vision will become clear only when you look into your own heart. Who looks outside, dreams. Who looks inside, awakes." Taking the time to reflect on what you have learned, what you did well, and what you would do differently brings about a unique awareness that will prepare you that much more to seize the opportunities ahead. Every seven days you will have a chance to "awaken" through the practice of reflection. Within this reflection time, there will be five areas of focus: *Wins, Opportunities, Steps to Success, Gratitude*, and *Insights & Inspirations*.

- *Wins:* Celebrating your *Wins* is just as important as anything else. Your *Wins* may include completing an extra action step within the 7-day period or receiving a compliment on the progress you are making. Maybe you want to share that day in which you only thought positively of yourself or brought joy to another. If it is a win to you, it is a win worth noting!
- *Opportunities:* Share the challenges or roadblocks you came across within the past seven days here. Did your Saboteur (that voice of negativity, blame, etc., that keeps us from achieving our goals) pay a visit? Were you hoping for something different to happen with a certain situation? Though at first glance these challenges may appear negative or daunting, they are actually opportunities. We are clear when something is working, but we also need to become aware of what is not working in order to make the necessary changes that lead to something better. These moments provide opportunities for growth, learning and boldness within the Adventure.
- *Steps to Success:* Take what you discover based on your *Wins* and *Opportunities* and apply the knowledge to the next seven days to achieve the most effective results. What steps can you take that will achieve a better outcome and bring you closer to achieving your 90-Day Goal faster and with greater fulfillment?
- *Gratitude:* Detail what you are grateful for and who you appreciate.
- *Insights & Inspirations:* Use this space for journal writing, vision explorations, doodles, and whatever else you deem appropriate for expressing your thoughts and feelings about your travels.

Reflection reminds us of our purpose and helps us really see and savor the positive changes we are making happen. When we take the time to think about what we learn along the way, we grow in our understanding and appreciation of what was experienced, opening the door to a much more enriching life. These reflective exercises are also quite powerful in firing up our creativity, resourcefulness, and expanded vision. As you experience the impact of reflection, feel free to note what comes from it within your *Reflections* pages, as well as *Insights & Inspirations*.

30-Day and 60-Day Milestone Reflections

Similar to the *7-Day Reflections*, the *30-Day* and *60-Day Milestone Reflections* include opportunities to explore what you have learned and how you will apply your newfound knowledge. These reflection pages also include the last two days of the 30-day segment and what action steps are left to take in order to reach the milestone. Consider those actions that must be completed in order for you to feel as though you have been successful on the first and second legs of your Adventure. Check off each action step as you complete it.

Within the *30-Day* and *60-Day Milestone Reflections* you will also find a space in which you can detail how you will reward yourself for reaching the milestone. Refer to what you wrote within your *Milestone Action Plan*. Just as every adventure needs moments for reflection, there is also a time for celebration and reward. This adventure is no different. Once you have completed your *30-Day* and *60-Day Milestones*, take some time to celebrate your accomplishments. You have worked hard to reach this point of the journey. Reward yourself and relish in the achievements.

90-Day Goal Reflection and Travel Writer Challenge

You have done it! You have reached your destination! To round out the journey you will have an opportunity to look back at how far you have come. What did you learn? How have you grown? What does it mean for you to have completed this quest? By the time you have reached the *90-Day Goal Reflection*, you will surely have a tale to tell that will inspire many. You are a true adventurer and you will find that there are people who want to know how you did it. What inspired you to take the journey in the first place? What motivated you to keep moving forward? Where will your travels take you next?

At the end of this Adventure, you will be presented with a very special request, in which you will be asked to step into the role of seasoned travel writer. The *Travel Writer Challenge* is your opportunity to inspire others with your story. In return, you will receive great reward, as well as a gift from me.

Now grab your pack and remember to play with possibility, enjoy the journey, and be bold in your pursuit!!!

Happy Adventures!!!

30-Day Milestone Action Plan		
Start date of milestone:		End date of milestone:
Within the next 30 days I will:		
To accomplish my 30-Day Milestone, I will take the following action steps:		

Events that may challenge me in successfully completing my 30-Day Milestone include:

I will take the following actions to face and conquer these potential challenges and roadblocks:

Special dates and events coming up within the next 30 days for my encouraging travel partners and supporters include:			
Partner/Supporter	Date	Event	To-Do

Mark these dates in your *Weekly Itinerary*.

30-Day Milestone Achievement Reward

I will reward myself for achieving my 30-Day Milestone in the following way:

"The secret of getting ahead is getting started."
~ Mark Twain ~

Week of:							
Day 1		**Day 2**		**Day 3**		**Day 4**	
6a							
7a							
8a							
9a							
10a							
11a							
12p							
1p							
2p							
3p							
4p							
5p							
6p							
7p							
8p							
9p							
10p							

Today I Will:

90-Day Goal

7-Day Action Steps

1	
2	
3	
4	

"As soon as I saw you, I knew an adventure was going to happen." Winnie the Pooh

Day 5		Day 6		Day 7		Confidence Booster Challenge
6a						**Choose a personal motto and create a motivational soundtrack for your journey** - A motto is a statement you live by. Draft a personal motto that resonates with and inspires you to move forward in your journey. Speak it out loud to remind yourself of your strength and value. Next, create a motivational soundtrack for your journey. I use Spotify (www.spotify.com), but you may choose to add the tracks to your iPod or a mixed CD. Continue to add to your soundtrack and play it often throughout your Adventure. (See next page.)
7a						
8a						
9a						
10a						
11a						
12p						
1p						
2p						
3p						
4p						
5p						
6p						
7p						
8p						
9p						
10p						

Today I Will:						Motivational Resources I Love!

Insights & Inspirations

Confidence Booster Challenge Journal

* My personal motto is:
* Songs on my motivational soundtrack include:
* Creating a personal motto and motivational soundtrack builds my confidence by:

What did the Confidence Booster Challenge bring forth for you?
What did you learn?

Confidence Booster Challenge Journal

Insights & Inspirations

7-Day Reflection
Wins - What did you do well?
Opportunities - Where are areas of growth and improvement?
Steps to Success - Knowing what you know now, what steps will you take in the next 7 days that will help you reach your 90-Day Goal?
Moments of Gratitude - What were you grateful for these last 7 days? Who were the travel partners that encouraged you? How did they support you?

Week of:							
Day 8		**Day 9**		**Day 10**		**Day 11**	
6a							
7a							
8a							
9a							
10a							
11a							
12p							
1p							
2p							
3p							
4p							
5p							
6p							
7p							
8p							
9p							
10p							

Today I Will:

90-Day Goal

7-Day Action Steps

1	
2	
3	
4	

	"Life begins at the end of your comfort zone." Neale Donald Walsch			
	Day 12	**Day 13**	**Day 14**	**Confidence Booster Challenge**
6a				**Name your Saboteur** - that internal voice of negativity, non-truths, etc. To best meet any challenge, we must first know our opponent. The Saboteur is a sly character, using trickery to keep us from achieving our best. Rather than indulge the ways of the Saboteur, seek to understand your inner critic. Name it, notice when it appears, and pay attention to how it works. Is there a pattern? What does it try to make you believe? When your Saboteur visits, say "Hi, (insert name here)! No time for you today. Be on your way." Then, continue on your journey. (See next page.)
7a				
8a				
9a				
10a				
11a				
12p				
1p				
2p				
3p				
4p				
5p				
6p				
7p				
8p				
9p				
10p				

Today I Will:			Motivational Resources I Love!

Insights & Inspirations

* The name of my Saboteur is:
* My Saboteur typically shows up when:
* My Saboteur tries to make me believe:
* My Saboteur keeps me from my best by using the following tricks:
* Knowing my Saboteur and its personality builds my confidence by:

What did the Confidence Booster Challenge bring forth for you?
What did you learn?

7-Day Reflection

Wins - What did you do well?

Opportunities - Where are areas of growth and improvement?

Steps to Success - Knowing what you know now, what steps will you take in the next 7 days that will help you reach your 90-Day Goal?

Moments of Gratitude - What were you grateful for these last 7 days? Who were the travel partners that encouraged you? How did they support you?

Week of:			
Day 15	**Day 16**	**Day 17**	**Day 18**
6a			
7a			
8a			
9a			
10a			
11a			
12p			
1p			
2p			
3p			
4p			
5p			
6p			
7p			
8p			
9p			
10p			

Today I Will:

90-Day Goal

7-Day Action Steps

1	
2	
3	
4	

"Somewhere, something incredible is waiting to be known." Carl Sagan

	Day 19	Day 20	Day 21	Confidence Booster Challenge
6a				**Share your Gifts** - You have so many gifts that are unique to you and those gifts are valued greatly by others. Consider all of the ways in which you contribute, and make the world a brighter place. In what way do you share your gifts? Are you creative? Do you always see the positive side of life? Are you good with kids? Take a step further and ask your travel partners and supporters: friends, family, peers, etc., what gifts they see in you. Continue to add to the list as you discover more great gifts and as others share with you how you make a difference. (See next page.)
7a				
8a				
9a				
10a				
11a				
12p				
1p				
2p				
3p				
4p				
5p				
6p				
7p				
8p				
9p				
10p				

Today I Will:

Motivational Resources I Love!

Insights & Inspirations

Confidence Booster Challenge Journal

* My gifts and the ways in which I contribute are:
* My travel partners and supporters say my gifts and contributions include:
* Recognizing my gifts and contributions builds my confidence by:

What did the Confidence Booster Challenge bring forth for you?
What did you learn?

7-Day Reflection
Wins - What did you do well?
Opportunities - Where are areas of growth and improvement?
Steps to Success - Knowing what you know now, what steps will you take in the next 7 days that will help you reach your 90-Day Goal?
Moments of Gratitude - What were you grateful for these last 7 days? Who were the travel partners that encouraged you? How did they support you?

Insights & Inspirations

Week of:			
Day 22	**Day 23**	**Day 24**	**Day 25**
6a			
7a			
8a			
9a			
10a			
11a			
12p			
1p			
2p			
3p			
4p			
5p			
6p			
7p			
8p			
9p			
10p			

Today I Will:

90-Day Goal

7-Day Action Steps

1	
2	
3	
4	

"The future belongs to those who believe in the beauty of their dreams." Eleanor Roosevelt			
Day 26	**Day 27**	**Day 28**	**Confidence Booster Challenge**
6a			**Educate & Prepare -** Boost your confidence and achieve your goals by educating and preparing yourself. Committing to these principles is especially helpful when trying something new. For example, say your goal is to run a marathon. Showing up to the starting line knowing little about running or the race itself may lead to falling short of the finish line. However, educating yourself about the course ahead and preparing your body to meet the challenge not only increases your probability of completing the race, but also your confidence. (See next page.)
7a			
8a			
9a			
10a			
11a			
12p			
1p			
2p			
3p			
4p			
5p			
6p			
7p			
8p			
9p			
10p			
Today I Will:			**Motivational Resources I Love!**
Insights & Inspirations			

Confidence Booster Challenge Journal

* The ways in which I am better educating and preparing myself so that I can meet my 90-Day Goal include:

* Educating and preparing myself builds my confidence by:

What did the Confidence Booster Challenge bring forth for you?
What did you learn?

7-Day Reflection

Wins - What did you do well?

Opportunities - Where are areas of growth and improvement?

Steps to Success - Knowing what you know now, what steps will you take in the next 7 days that will help you reach your 90-Day Goal?

Moments of Gratitude - What were you grateful for these last 7 days? Who were the travel partners that encouraged you? How did they support you?

Insights & Inspirations

Week of:			
Day 29		**Day 30**	**90-Day Goal**
6a			
7a			
8a			
9a			**30-Day Milestone**
10a			
11a			
12p			
1p			
2p			**Remaining Actions to Take to**
3p			**Achieve 30-Day Milestone:**
4p			
5p			
6p			
7p			
8p			
9p			
10p			
Today I Will:			
What accomplishments have you made within the last 30 days?			
30-Day Milestone Achievement Reward			

46

30-Day Milestone Reflection
Wins – What did you do well in the last 30 days?
Opportunities – What are areas of growth or improvement you have seen in the last 30 days?
Steps to Success - Knowing what you know now, what steps will you take in the next 30 days that will help you reach your 90-Day Goal?
Moments of Gratitude - What were you grateful for these last 30 days? Who were the travel partners that encouraged you? How did they support you?
What have you learned on the journey so far?
Now, go celebrate your success!!!
"The heart of human excellence begins to beat when you discover a pursuit that absorbs you, frees you, challenges you, or gives you a sense of meaning, joy or passion." ~ Terry Orlick ~

60-Day Milestone Action Plan		
Start date of milestone:		End date of milestone:
Within the next 30 days I will:		
To accomplish my 60-Day Milestone, I will take the following action steps:		

Events that may challenge me in successfully completing my 60-Day Milestone include:			

I will take the following actions to face and conquer these potential challenges and roadblocks:

Special dates and events coming up within the next 30 days for my encouraging travel partners and supporters include:			
Partner/Supporter	Date	Event	To-Do

Mark these dates in your *Weekly Itinerary.*

60-Day Milestone Achievement Reward

I will reward myself for achieving my 60-Day Milestone in the following way:

"The real voyage of discovery consists not in seeking new landscapes but in having new eyes."
~ Marcel Proust ~

Week of:			
Day 31	**Day 32**	**Day 33**	**Day 34**
6a			
7a			
8a			
9a			
10a			
11a			
12p			
1p			
2p			
3p			
4p			
5p			
6p			
7p			
8p			
9p			
10p			

Today I Will:

90-Day Goal

7-Day Action Steps

1	
2	
3	
4	

"Hardships often prepare ordinary people for extraordinary destiny." C.S. Lewis			
Day 35	**Day 36**	**Day 37**	**Confidence Booster Challenge**
6a			**Clear the Clutter** – Whether the clutter is physical, mental, or both, the mess of it all can cause both your focus and your confidence to waver, keeping you from achieving your best. Clear the physical clutter by cleaning your surroundings - desk, home, car, etc. – and adding motivating cues (i.e. inspirational quotes to the mirror). Clear the mental clutter by letting go of the thoughts, beliefs and limitations - yours and others - that hold you back. Fill your mind only with thoughts – yours and others - that inspire you and keep you moving forward. (See next page.)
7a			
8a			
9a			
10a			
11a			
12p			
1p			
2p			
3p			
4p			
5p			
6p			
7p			
8p			
9p			
10p			
Today I Will:			**Motivational Resources I Love!**
Insights & Inspirations			

Confidence Booster Challenge Journal

* I am clearing my physical clutter by:
* I am clearing my mental clutter by:
* Clearing my physical and mental clutter builds my confidence by:

What did the Confidence Booster Challenge bring forth for you?
What did you learn?

7-Day Reflection
Wins - What did you do well?
Opportunities - Where are areas of growth and improvement?
Steps to Success - Knowing what you know now, what steps will you take in the next 7 days that will help you reach your 90-Day Goal?
Moments of Gratitude - What were you grateful for these last 7 days? Who were the travel partners that encouraged you? How did they support you?

Insights & Inspirations

Week of:			
Day 38	**Day 39**	**Day 40**	**Day 41**
6a			
7a			
8a			
9a			
10a			
11a			
12p			
1p			
2p			
3p			
4p			
5p			
6p			
7p			
8p			
9p			
10p			

Today I Will:

90-Day Goal

7-Day Action Steps

1	
2	
3	
4	

	Day 42	Day 43	Day 44	Confidence Booster Challenge
6a				**Be of Service** - Giving back to others and our communities provides an unmatched confidence and reward. We are truly our best selves when we are serving others. Being of service may be as simple as returning a smile or buying someone a cup of coffee. Other ways to be of service include sharing your gifts, volunteering your time, and showing kindness wherever possible. Not feeling in a giving mood? This is simply a prompt to get out there and give even more. You will not only make someone else's day, but you will turn yours around also.\n\n(See next page.)
7a				
8a				
9a				
10a				
11a				
12p				
1p				
2p				
3p				
4p				
5p				
6p				
7p				
8p				
9p				
10p				

Today I Will:			Motivational Resources I Love!

Insights & Inspirations

Confidence Booster Challenge Journal

* I am being of service by:
* Being of service builds my confidence by:

What did the Confidence Booster Challenge bring forth for you?
What did you learn?

Insights & Inspirations

7-Day Reflection
Wins - What did you do well?
Opportunities - Where are areas of growth and improvement?
Steps to Success - Knowing what you know now, what steps will you take in the next 7 days that will help you reach your 90-Day Goal?
Moments of Gratitude - What were you grateful for these last 7 days? Who were the travel partners that encouraged you? How did they support you?

Week of:			
Day 45	**Day 46**	**Day 47**	**Day 48**

	Day 45		Day 46		Day 47		Day 48
6a							
7a							
8a							
9a							
10a							
11a							
12p							
1p							
2p							
3p							
4p							
5p							
6p							
7p							
8p							
9p							
10p							

Today I Will:

90-Day Goal

7-Day Action Steps

1	
2	
3	
4	

	Day 49	Day 50	Day 51	Confidence Booster Challenge
6a				**Act "As If"** - Act as though you already have achieved your 90-Day Goal. Think about it. If you were already at the end of your Adventure, what would you be doing right now? How would your life be different? Play the role. The more you act "as if," the more real the feelings and experience will become. For example, you may want to conquer your fear of public speaking. Act as though you are already the best public speaker out there. How would you deliver your message? Imagine how confident you would feel. Give your talk with this vision in mind. (See next page.)
7a				
8a				
9a				
10a				
11a				
12p				
1p				
2p				
3p				
4p				
5p				
6p				
7p				
8p				
9p				
10p				

Today I Will:			Motivational Resources I Love!

Insights & Inspirations

Confidence Booster Challenge Journal

* The areas of my life in which I would like to be more confident are:
* I acted "as if" when:
* Acting "as if" builds my confidence by:

What did the Confidence Booster Challenge bring forth for you?
What did you learn?

7-Day Reflection
Wins - What did you do well?
Opportunities - Where are areas of growth and improvement?
Steps to Success - Knowing what you know now, what steps will you take in the next 7 days that will help you reach your 90-Day Goal?
Moments of Gratitude - What were you grateful for these last 7 days? Who were the travel partners that encouraged you? How did they support you?

Insights & Inspirations

Week of:			
Day 52	**Day 53**	**Day 54**	**Day 55**
6a			
7a			
8a			
9a			
10a			
11a			
12p			
1p			
2p			
3p			
4p			
5p			
6p			
7p			
8p			
9p			
10p			

Today I Will:			

90-Day Goal

7-Day Action Steps	
1	
2	
3	
4	

"You are far too smart to be the only thing standing in your way." Jennifer Freeman

	Day 56	Day 57	Day 58	Confidence Booster Challenge
6a				**Stand Tall and Get Moving** - Paying attention to and taking care of your body can ignite a powerful confidence. Start with focusing on your posture. Stand tall. Sit tall. There are many reasons to hold your head up high. Look at how far you have come and think about what you are about to accomplish. You are amazing! Next, get moving. Exercise! Take a walk. Try out a kickboxing class. Notice how great you feel and remember with every lunge and sit-up, you are not only building a stronger core, but a greater confidence.

(See next page.) |
7a				
8a				
9a				
10a				
11a				
12p				
1p				
2p				
3p				
4p				
5p				
6p				
7p				
8p				
9p				
10p				

Today I Will:

Motivational Resources I Love!

Insights & Inspirations

69

* I get my body moving by:
* Paying attention to my posture and taking care of my body builds my confidence by:

What did the Confidence Booster Challenge bring forth for you?
What did you learn?

7-Day Reflection
Wins - What did you do well?
Opportunities - Where are areas of growth and improvement?
Steps to Success - Knowing what you know now, what steps will you take in the next 7 days that will help you reach your 90-Day Goal?
Moments of Gratitude - What were you grateful for these last 7 days? Who were the travel partners that encouraged you? How did they support you?

Insights & Inspirations

	Week of:		90-Day Goal
Day 59		**Day 60**	
6a			
7a			
8a			
9a			**60-Day Milestone**
10a			
11a			
12p			
1p			
2p			**Remaining Actions to Take to Achieve 60-Day Milestone:**
3p			
4p			
5p			
6p			
7p			
8p			
9p			
10p			
Today I Will:			

What accomplishments have you made within the last 30 days?

60-Day Milestone Achievement Reward

60-Day Milestone Reflection
Wins – What did you do well in the last 30 days?
Opportunities – What are areas of growth or improvement you have seen in the last 30 days?
Steps to Success - Knowing what you know now, what steps will you take in the next 30 days that will help you reach your 90-Day Goal?
Moments of Gratitude - What were you grateful for these last 30 days? Who were the travel partners that encouraged you? How did they support you?
What have you learned on the journey so far?
Now, go celebrate your success!!!
"We begin to find and become ourselves when we notice how we are already found, already truly, entirely, wildly, messily, marvelously, who we were born to be."   ~ Anne Lamott ~

	Homestretch *(final 30 days)* Action Plan
End date of 90-Day Goal:	

Within the next 30 days I will:

To accomplish my 90-Day Goal, I will take the following action steps:

Events that may challenge me in successfully completing my 90-Day Goal include:			

I will take the following actions to face and conquer these potential challenges and roadblocks:			

Special dates and events coming up within the next 30 days for my encouraging travel partners and supporters include:			
Partner/Supporter	Date	Event	To-Do

Mark these dates in your *Weekly Itinerary*.

90-Day Goal Achievement Reward

I will reward myself for achieving my 90-Day Goal in the following way:

"What do dreams know of boundaries?"
~ Amelia Earheart ~

	Week of:						
	Day 61		**Day 62**		**Day 63**		**Day 64**
6a							
7a							
8a							
9a							
10a							
11a							
12p							
1p							
2p							
3p							
4p							
5p							
6p							
7p							
8p							
9p							
10p							

Today I Will:

90-Day Goal

7-Day Action Steps

1	
2	
3	
4	

"Nothing is impossible. The word itself says, 'I'm possible!'" Audrey Hepburn			
Day 65	**Day 66**	**Day 67**	**Confidence Booster Challenge**

	Day 65	Day 66	Day 67	Confidence Booster Challenge
6a				**Focus on Learning & Practice** - Letting go of the need to be perfect can free you to be more creative, joyful, and successful. Instead of second-guessing yourself at every turn, wondering if you are good enough, or trying to make others happy, take each step with a desire to learn & practice. When we are learning & practicing, failure does not exist. Consider a baby as they explore the world. They do not fear making mistakes and do not try for perfection. Instead they focus on learning & practicing, building new skills step by step until they have been mastered, achieving their goal.

(See next page.) |
7a				
8a				
9a				
10a				
11a				
12p				
1p				
2p				
3p				
4p				
5p				
6p				
7p				
8p				
9p				
10p				

Today I Will:			**Motivational Resources I Love!**

Insights & Inspirations	

Confidence Booster Challenge Journal

* I am learning:

* I am practicing new skills by:

* Focusing on learning and practice helps build my confidence by:

What did the Confidence Booster Challenge bring forth for you?
What did you learn?

7-Day Reflection

Wins - What did you do well?

Opportunities - Where are areas of growth and improvement?

Steps to Success - Knowing what you know now, what steps will you take in the next 7 days that will help you reach your 90-Day Goal?

Moments of Gratitude - What were you grateful for these last 7 days? Who were the travel partners that encouraged you? How did they support you?

Insights & Inspirations

Week of:							
Day 68		**Day 69**		**Day 70**		**Day 71**	
6a							
7a							
8a							
9a							
10a							
11a							
12p							
1p							
2p							
3p							
4p							
5p							
6p							
7p							
8p							
9p							
10p							

Today I Will:

90-Day Goal

7-Day Action Steps

1	
2	
3	
4	

"Fear has two meanings: 'Forget everything and run' or 'Face everything and rise.' The choice is yours." Zig Ziglar

	Day 72	Day 73	Day 74	Confidence Booster Challenge
6a				**Take a Risk** - Do something that scares you or fills you with nervous excitement every time you consider taking action. What have you always wanted to do, but haven't because of fear? Do it! Remember your Saboteur? What was the name? Your Saboteur thrives on fear. How is your Saboteur holding you back? How will you defy your Saboteur today? Be a rebel. Be bold in your pursuit of something amazing. Facing our fears builds our confidence by moving us outside of our comfort zone and showing us what we are fully capable of. You can do this! (See next page.)
7a				
8a				
9a				
10a				
11a				
12p				
1p				
2p				
3p				
4p				
5p				
6p				
7p				
8p				
9p				
10p				

Today I Will:

Motivational Resources I Love!

Insights & Inspirations

Confidence Booster Challenge Journal

* What I am not doing in my life because of fear is:
* I took the following risk(s), showing my Saboteur that I am not listening today:
* Taking the risk(s) builds my confidence by:

What did the Confidence Booster Challenge bring forth for you?
What did you learn?

7-Day Reflection
Wins - What did you do well?
Opportunities - Where are areas of growth and improvement?
Steps to Success - Knowing what you know now, what steps will you take in the next 7 days that will help you reach your 90-Day Goal?
Moments of Gratitude - What were you grateful for these last 7 days? Who were the travel partners that encouraged you? How did they support you?

Insights & Inspirations

Week of:			
Day 75	**Day 76**	**Day 77**	**Day 78**
6a			
7a			
8a			
9a			
10a			
11a			
12p			
1p			
2p			
3p			
4p			
5p			
6p			
7p			
8p			
9p			
10p			

Today I Will:

90-Day Goal

7-Day Action Steps

1	
2	
3	
4	

"Make visible what without you might perhaps never have been seen." Robert Breeson

	Day 79		Day 80		Day 81	Confidence Booster Challenge
6a						**Get Creative!** – Do you want to write a song, paint a masterpiece, or dance on Broadway? Take some time to indulge your creative self! Creativity can not only unleash your imagination, but standing back to see what you completed can be a major confidence booster. Coming up with new ideas and solutions and developing them is also a wonderful way to get creative. When you get creative, you welcome new possibilities. Explore what you have within, invest in your uniqueness and share your gifts. The world is waiting for what you are creating!
7a						
8a						
9a						
10a						
11a						
12p						
1p						
2p						
3p						
4p						
5p						
6p						
7p						
8p						
9p						
10p						(See next page.)

Today I Will:

Motivational Resources I Love!

Insights & Inspirations

Confidence Booster Challenge Journal

* I am celebrating my creativity by:
* Getting creative builds my confidence by:

What did the Confidence Booster Challenge bring forth for you?
What did you learn?

7-Day Reflection
Wins - What did you do well?
Opportunities - Where are areas of growth and improvement?
Steps to Success - Knowing what you know now, what steps will you take in the next 7 days that will help you reach your 90-Day Goal?
Moments of Gratitude - What were you grateful for these last 7 days? Who were the travel partners that encouraged you? How did they support you?

Insights & Inspirations

Week of:							
Day 82		**Day 83**		**Day 84**		**Day 85**	
6a							
7a							
8a							
9a							
10a							
11a							
12p							
1p							
2p							
3p							
4p							
5p							
6p							
7p							
8p							
9p							
10p							

Today I Will:

90-Day Goal

7-Day Action Steps

1	
2	
3	
4	

"I am not what has happened to me. I am what I choose to become." Carl Jung			
Day 86	**Day 87**	**Day 88**	**Confidence Booster Challenge**
6a			**Try Something New** - It could be anything. Ride a bike to your destination in place of driving, go parasailing, try out a new dish or coffee flavor, visit an attraction you have yet to see - the list goes on. There is a great world to explore. Invite discovery into your daily life. Prioritize boldness in place of fear. Invest in the experience. Enjoy every moment. Choose to take on the world with curiosity and courage. Trying new things creates opportunities for understanding, growth and greater confidence, while also leading to a life of adventure. (See next page.)
7a			
8a			
9a			
10a			
11a			
12p			
1p			
2p			
3p			
4p			
5p			
6p			
7p			
8p			
9p			
10p			
Today I Will:			**Motivational Resources I Love!**
Insights & Inspirations			

Confidence Booster Challenge Journal

* Some new things I am trying include:
* Trying new things builds my confidence by:

What did the Confidence Booster Challenge bring forth for you?
What did you learn?

7-Day Reflection
Wins - What did you do well?
Opportunities - Where are areas of growth and improvement?
Steps to Success - Knowing what you know now, what steps will you take in the next 7 days that will help you reach your 90-Day Goal?
Moments of Gratitude - What were you grateful for these last 7 days? Who were the travel partners that encouraged you? How did they support you?

	Week of:		
	Day 89	**Day 90**	**90-Day Goal**
6a			
7a			
8a			
9a			**Remaining Actions to Take to Complete My**
10a			**Brightside 90-Day Goal Adventure:**
11a			
12p			
1p			
2p			
3p			
4p			
5p			
6p			
7p			
8p			
9p			
10p			
	Today I Will:		
What accomplishments have you made within the last 30 days?			
90-Day Goal Achievement Reward			

90-Day Goal Reflection

What did you learn on your journey?

What are you most proud of?

How has your life changed since beginning your 90-Day Goal Adventure?

What does accomplishing your 90-Day Goal mean to you?

What Adventure will you take next?

Now, go celebrate your success!!!

"We are at our very best, and we are happiest, when we are fully engaged in work we enjoy on the journey toward the goal we've established for ourselves. It gives meaning to our time off and comfort to our sleep. It makes everything else in life so wonderful, so worthwhile."

~ Earl Nightingale ~

Brightside 90-Day Goal Adventure Achieved!

"Life is pure adventure and as soon as we realize that, the quicker we will be able to treat life as art."
Maya Angelou

Congratulations! You've done it! You have achieved your Brightside 90-Day Goal Adventure! This was a challenging quest, and yet, you completed the journey.

Thank you for taking this Adventure and living your life inspired while inspiring others. You are a true hero, taking bold steps to create a life filled with joy, excitement and fulfillment. I hope you will take the time to celebrate this remarkable accomplishment and reflect upon all that you have learned about yourself along the way. Celebrate BIG! You have earned it!

I also invite you to share your glory with your travel partners and supporters, the Brightside 90-Day Goal Adventurers, and with me! I want to hear all about your Adventure! This is your moment to shine and I would love to celebrate your success right alongside you! Step into the role of seasoned travel writer with the *Travel Writer Challenge* and tell your tale by sharing your Adventure with a picture of yourself at www.brightsidecareer.com. Tell me about the 90-Day Goal you chose, where you started in this journey, the wins, the opportunities, what you learned along the way, and anything else that you want to highlight. I am excited to hear all about it! And, when you do, I have a *special celebration gift just for you*.

I look forward to meeting back up with you when you are ready to take on your next Brightside 90-Day Goal Adventure. Until then, enjoy celebrating what you have achieved and always remember to *adventure in possibility*. See you soon!

Your Fellow Brightside 90-Day Goal Adventurer,

Helen

■ ■

FOR MORE RESOURCES AND INFORMATION ABOUT BUSINESS AND CAREER COACHING WITH HELEN, VISIT WWW.BRIGHTSIDECAREER.COM.

FOR MORE INFORMATION ABOUT FREELANCE EDITING AND WRITING SERVICES, VISIT WWW.ANDREWFICKES.COM.

Made in the USA
San Bernardino, CA
30 December 2015